SWANSEA TO CARMARTHEN

Vic Mitchell and Keith Smith

MP Middleton Press

Front cover: Leaving platform 3 at Carmarthen in August 1952 is 2-6-0 no. 6331. Part of the engine shed is on the right, this housing almost 50 locomotives. (M.Whitehouse coll.)

Back cover: Cwmmawr Opencast Disposal Sidings were recorded on 25th May 1995 with no. 08993 undertaking the shunting. (H.Ballantyne)

**Published to mark the centenary of
the first passenger trains on the
Burry Port & Gwendraeth Valley Railway.**

Published September 2009

ISBN 978 1 906008 59 8

© Middleton Press, 2009

Design Deborah Esher
Typesetting Barbara Mitchell

Published by
        Middleton Press
        Easebourne Lane
        Midhurst
        West Sussex
        GU29 9AZ
Tel: 01730 813169
Fax: 01730 812601
Email: info@middletonpress.co.uk
www.middletonpress.co.uk

Printed in the United Kingdom by Henry Ling Limited, at the Dorset Press, Dorchester, DT1 1HD

CONTENTS

INDEX

ACKNOWLEDGEMENTS

We are very grateful for the assistance received from many of those mentioned in the credits also to P.G.Barnes, A.R.Carder, R.Caston, L.Crosier, G.Croughton, A.Davies, S.C.Jenkins, P.Kelley, J.Langford, N.Langridge, B.Lewis, Mr D. and Dr S.Salter, N.W.Sprinks, T.Walsh, E.Wilmshurst and in particular, our always supportive wives, Barbara Mitchell and Janet Smith.

I. GWR map for 1947, with passenger routes shown as solid black lines.

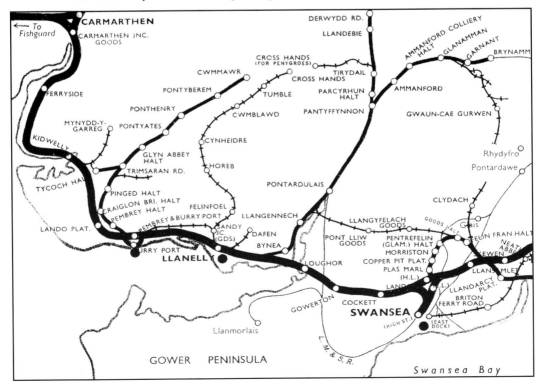

GEOGRAPHICAL SETTING

Swansea had for long been pre-eminent in the field of non-ferrous metal processing, having the advantage of being surrounded by productive coal measures. These stretch west to Pembrey, their boundary being northeast thereof, along the valley of the Gwendraeth Fawr. This end of the coalfield is noted for the production of anthracite of high calorific value. Northwest of this valley is a ridge of limestone, which runs towards the Black Mountain.

Apart from climbing out of the Tawe Valley and descending into the Llan Valley on leaving Swansea, the main line is mostly level, being on the coastal plain. The final few miles run in the tidal part of the Towy Valley, on the approach to Carmarthen. It is probably the oldest recorded town in Wales, a Roman fort being listed in AD75.

The maps are to the scale of 25ins to 1 mile, with north at the top, unless otherwise indicated. The Welsh spelling and hyphenation has varied over the years and we have generally used the most recent form, as have the railways.

Gradient profile, with the mileage from London via the Severn Tunnel.

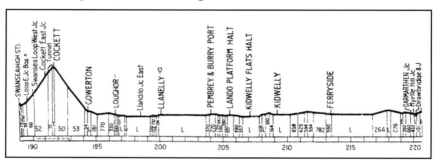

HISTORICAL BACKGROUND

The first main line in the area was that of the South Wales Railway, which opened between Chepstow and Swansea on 19th June 1850 and became part of the Great Western Railway in 1862. It was broad gauge (7ft 0¼ins) until May 1872.

The route was extended from Landore to Carmarthen (later Junction station) on 11th October 1852 and leased to the GWR forthwith. It was double track to Pembrey and the remainder was doubled in February 1853. The route was extended to Haverfordwest in 1854 and a branch to Carmarthen Town opened on 1st March 1860. It ran north to Conwil and was part of the Carmarthen & Cardigan Railway until 1881. A line from Llandeilo joined it in 1864.

An earlier local line was that of the Llanelly Railway & Dock Company, which ran north to Pontardulais from 1839. It became part of the GWR in 1889. Running south from that town to Swansea via Gowerton and the coast was the LR & D's 1865 route. After a number of owners, it became London & North Western Railway property in 1891 and London Midland & Scottish in 1923.

The GWR lasted until nationalisation in 1948, when its routes became part of the Western Region of British Railways. Privatisation in 1996 resulted in South Wales & West providing services ("South" was dropped in 1998). However, after reorganisation in 2001, Wales & Borders became the franchisee. Arriva Trains Wales took over in December 2003.

London services were provided by Great Western Trains from 4th February 1996, this changing to First Great Western on 1st April 2006.

Station closures and freight withdrawals are given in the captions.

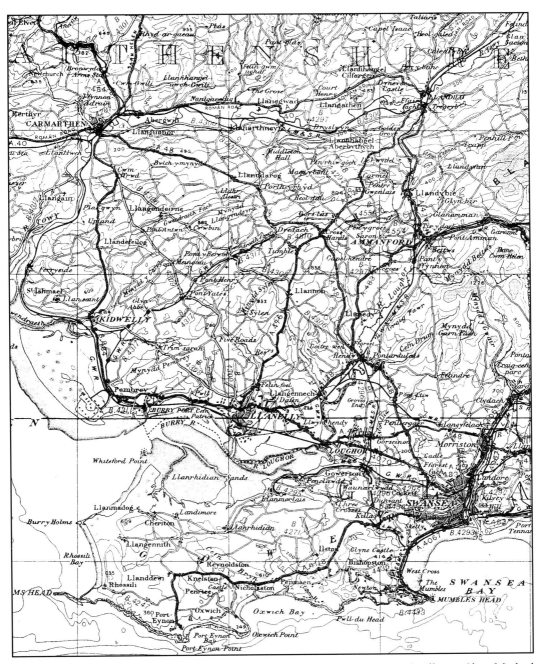

II.   Our route runs from lower right to top left on this 1946 survey at 4 miles to 1ins. Marked LM&SR, the route from the north into Swansea arrived in 1860 and closed to passengers in 1950.

Burry Port & Gwendraeth Valley Railway

The Kidwelly & Llanelly Canal & Tramroad Company received its Act on 20th June 1812, but its opening date and gauge are not known. The latter was probably 4ft 2ins and canal completion was around 1837. This was converted to a railway, albeit with very steep gradients near the sites of the locks, under an Act of 5th July 1865 and the name became the Kidwelly & Burry Port Railway. An enlarged undertaking was created with an Act on 30th April 1866 and was called the Burry Port & Gwendraeth Valley Railway. Mineral traffic began in June 1869 and many lines to collieries were built later.

A branch of the BP & GVR was opened to Kidwelly Quay in 1873, but bankruptcy followed from 1881 to 1898. Miners were carried from 1899 and this led to a Light Railway Order, with the help of H.F.Stephens, later known as "The Colonel". A public service began between Burry Port and Pontyberem on 2nd August 1909 and it was extended to Cwmmawr on 29th January 1913. The railway became part of the GWR on 1st July 1922 and its Quay line closed in October 1929. Passenger trains were withdrawn on 21st September 1953 and general goods traffic ceased on 12th July 1965. Coal traffic continued, but the Kidwelly Junction - Kidwelly part closed in 1965. It reopened in 1983, when the section south to Burry Port was closed. The Trimsaran branch (centre on map III) was in use from 1869 to 1962 and the line to Cwm Capel Colliery (below it) carried coal between about 1852 and 1940. The section between Burry Port and Pwll was used in 1891-1962 and east to Sandy Junction carried traffic in 1897-1967. Kidwelly to Cwmmawr closed in 1996.

III.   The Llanelly & Mynydd Mawr Railway was opened in 1883 and the line was closed north of Cynheidre Colliery (beyond the border of the map) in 1966 and south thereof in 1989. The Gwendraeth Valleys Railway opened in 1871 and the line was in use until 1960. The railways were absorbed by the GWR in 1922 and 1923 respectively. (Railway Magazine)

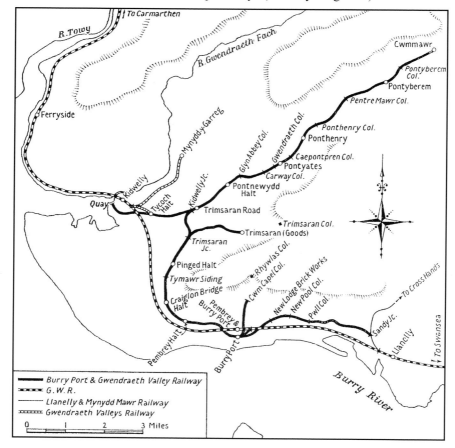

1. The locomotives of the BP&GVR ranged widely and only the extremes are shown. Initially there were two inadequate 0-4-0STs from Henry Hughes & Co. This early Fairlie 0-4-4-0 was completed in December 1869 and was a success, running until 1891.
(A.Dudman coll.)

2. Three 0-6-6-0s were built by James Cross & Co. in 1873 and became export rejects. They were rebuilt by the Yorkshire Engine Co. and one was obtained that year. Named *Victoria*, it lasted until 1892 and was equally successful.
(A.Dudman coll.)

3. The GWR inherited 15 0-6-0s with various tank types in 1922. Seven were still in use in 1953 and this Avonside product of 1900 is illustrated, as it survives to this day. Named *Pontyberem*, it was sold in 1913 and had a varied career. It was purchased for the Great Western Society in 1970 and subsequently has mostly resided at Didcot, being the only remaining BP&GVR engine.
(A.Dudman coll.)

PASSENGER SERVICES

Swansea to Carmarthen

The table below is intended to give an indication of the development of services. In some cases, a few of the faster trains ran from Landore and not Swansea, as they formed part of a long distance run. Short journeys and ones on less than five days per week are not included.

	Weekdays		Sundays	
	Most stations	Semi-fast	Most stations	Semi-fast
1870	5	2	2	1
1890	4	3	2	1
1910	8	7	2	1
1930	8	5	0	2
1950	12	6	0	5
1970	11	2	3	3
1990	11	4	4	4

Burry Port & Gwendraeth Valley

The majority of timetables showed four trains up the valley and five down. This train description was used after 1913, contrary to normal practice, where up refers to the London direction. The timetables showed a remarkable consistency.

BURRY PORT and CWMMAWR (One class only)

Miles	Up HOUR aft	8		1	S 5	S 9	E 9			Miles	Down HOUR aft	7		12	3		4	S 6	S 10	E 10
—	Burry Port.........dep.	10	.	45	50	20	30	. .	. .	—	Cwmmawr.........dep.	10	.	0	10	15	45	15	45	.
1¼	Pembrey Halt.........	15	.	50	55	25	35	. .	. .	2	Pontyberem	18	.	6	18	21	51	21	53	.
2¼	Craiglon Bridge Halt...	18	.	53	58	28	38	. .	. .	4	Ponthenry	25	.	13	28	28	58	28	0	.
3¼	Pinged Halt............	23	.	58	3	33	43	. .	. .	5	Pontyates.............	28	.	16	31	31	1	31	5	.
5	Trimsaran Road.........	30	.	5	8	39	49	. .	. .	7	Glyn Abbey.............	36	.	21	39	36	6	36	13	.
6	Glyn Abbey............	35	.	10	13	44	54	. .	. .	8	Trimsaran Road.........	41	.	26	45	41	11	41	20	.
8	Pontyates.............	41	.	18	19	50	2	. .	. .	9¾	Pinged Halt............	47	.	32	52	47	17	47	26	.
9	Ponthenry	44	.	21	22	53	5	. .	. .	10¾	Craiglon Bridge Halt ...	52	.	37	57	52	22	52	31	.
11	Pontyberem	51	.	30	29	0	14	. .	. .	11¾	Pembrey Halt	55	.	40	0	55	25	55	34	.
13	Cwmmawr G......arr.	57	.	38	35	6	22	. .	. .	13	Burry Port H 64, 69 arr	0	.	45	5	0	30	0	39	.

A Cathays (Woodville Rd) Halt   **B** Maindy (North Rd) Halt   **D** Sta for St Lawrence (Pembroke)   **E** Except Sats
    F Sta for St David's (13 mls)   **F** Fridays and Saturday only   **G** Sta for Tumble
    H Adjoins Pembrey and Burry Port Sta   **H** Except Fridays and Saturdays   **M** One class only
  N Dep Neyland 9 mrn, page 70   **P** 1st and 3rd class   **S** Sats. only   **V** Arr Neyland 8 47 mrn, page 64

Where the MINUTES under the Hours change to a LOWER figure and DARKER type it indicates the NEXT HOUR

August 1940

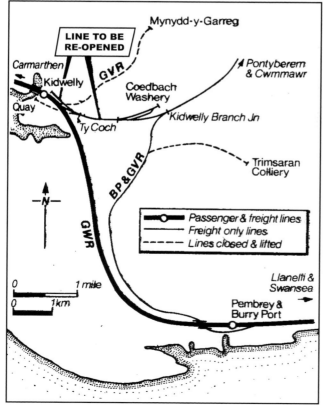

IV. This map shows the changes of 1983, together with the initials of the earlier owners. (Railway Magazine)

1. Swansea to Carmarthen

SWANSEA HIGH STREET

V.   The 1938 edition at 6ins to 1 mile has the terminus a little above centre. The LMS lines and its St. Thomas's Station are to the right of the River Tawe, while its Victoria terminus is above South Dock. This is illustrated in the *Llandeilo to Swansea* album, as is the Swansea & Mumbles Railway, the terminus of which is above the nearby goods shed.

4.   High Street Signal Box was otherwise known as No. 6 Cabin and was in use until 1926, when extensive rebuilding of the station took place. Initially there were two platforms, but there were four by 1879 and a short bay followed later, on the west side. (Lens of Sutton coll.)

5.   Most long distance trains to and from Carmarthen reversed here. This is the 7.30am Carmarthen to Paddington on 8th July 1947, having received a fresh engine, no. 5093 *Upton Castle*. Most boat trains carrying passengers to and from Ireland did not call here. (H.C.Casserley)

6.   A new frontage was completed in 1927 and it was photographed in 1958. This architectural style was employed further east at Newport and north at Aberystwyth. (Lens of Sutton coll.)

7.   Recorded on 29th June 1962 was 0-6-0PT no. 9792 waiting to take empty stock out to the carriage sidings. The disc under the roof is a "banner repeater", used on curved platforms when starting signals are obscured. (B.W.L.Brooksbank)

8.   The multitude of starting signals impressed the photographer on 27th September 1965. The massive goods shed is in the centre background, while the signal box is on the right. It closed on 14th October 1973. (R.F.Roberts/SLS)

SWANSEA

9.   The suffix "High Street" was lost on 6th May 1968, as the other termini had closed by that time. No. 47500 is about to leave with the 07.45 Cardiff to Milford Haven service. (P.Jones)

Other views of this station are to be found in our
Cardiff to Swansea **album.**

10.   DMU no. 944 formed the 11.35 to Pembroke Dock on 16th September 1990; an HST on a
London service waits on the right. (M.J.Stretton)

NORTH OF SWANSEA

← VI. The 1954 survey at 2ins to 1 mile shows closed stations with open circles and those then in use are grey. The High Street terminus is rectangular. North of it, the tracks diverge at Swansea East Junction, the 1850 one continuing north to Landore, which is just beyond the border. Curving left is the Swansea Loop, which opened to goods on 5th March 1906 and passengers on 1st May following. Across the top is the 1852 main line to West Wales. The dashed line is the Swansea & Mumbles Railway of 1807.

← 11. Swansea Loop East box is seen in September 1963, looking south, with the 1850 route in the foreground and the 1906 one curving behind the box. It was in use from 1907 until 14th October 1973 and had a 68-lever frame. (P.J.Garland/R.S.Carpenter)

12. Swansea Loop West Junction was photographed on 21st October 1982, looking west from the signal box. It was rebuilt in 1941 following bomb damage; the frame had 31 levers and was in use until 1973. The train will descend at 1 in 60 to East Junction. (T.Heavyside)

COCKETT

MARTELL STREET

Cockett Station

VII.   A climb at mostly 1 in 52 takes the line up to the 788yd-long Cockett Tunnel (right) and it continues at 1 in 71 through it. The 1915 survey at 20ins to 1 mile shows earthworks ready (top left) for a new goods line. The trackbed had been used for a siding to Worcester Wigfach and Cwmbach Collieries prior to 1899. The station first appeared in timetables in May 1871.

Tunnel
Brick Works
Clay Pit

Cockett	1903	1913	1923	1933
Passenger tickets issued	23830	42678	25081	16324
Season tickets issued	*	*	285	177
Parcels forwarded	1868	2724	5115	22103
General goods forwarded (tons)	12	35	120	1102
Coal and coke received (tons)	-	-	5135	5287
Other minerals received (tons)	3	1910	1703	767
General goods received (tons)	84	336	1120	1791
Coal and Coke handled	-	-	1307	6303
Trucks of livestock handled	108	94	31	20

* Not Available

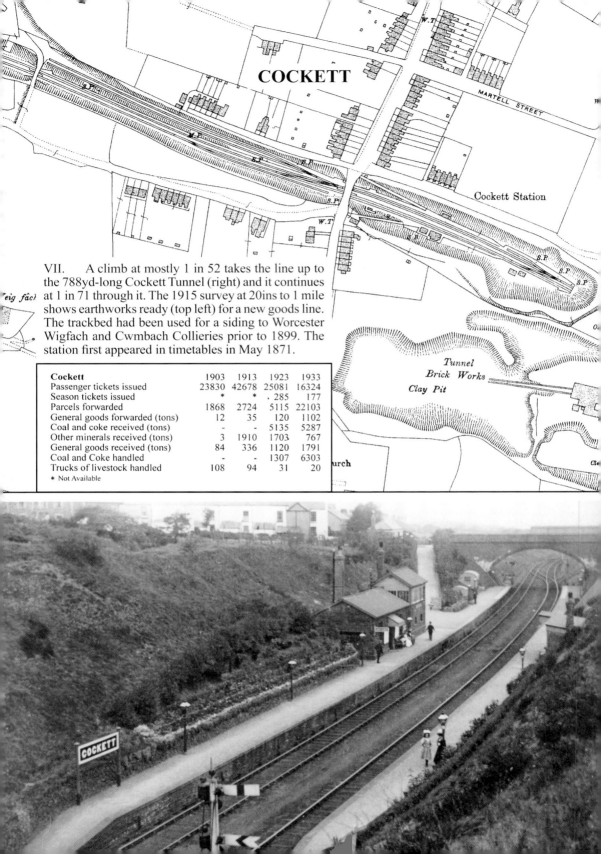

COCKETT

13. A westward panorama in the 1920s features the well sheltered gardens. The staff numbered 15 in 1913, this dropping to 9 by 1936. There was a down goods loop nearly a mile further west, in 1911-26. (M.Dart coll.)

14. A view east includes the short up siding, which was regularly used by banking locomotives awaiting return to Landore. The local population was 6125 in 1901; it grew substantially subsequently. (Stations UK)

15. Calling on 11th July 1958 is 0-6-0PT no. 8788 with the 4.57pm Kidwelly to Swansea stopping train. On the left is another short siding for use by banking engines. (H.C.Casserley)

16.   Turning round on the same day, we see both inclined approach paths, plus the lamp hut. The 25-lever signal box was in use from 1882 until 24th January 1966, by which time banking engines had become a thing of the past and their sidings soon vanished. (H.C.Casserley)

17.   The bridge is at the summit of the climb from the west and from it rises the line to the goods depot. This was used from 17th May 1915 to 13th September 1965. Passenger trains ceased to call on 15th June 1964. (P.J.Garland/R.S.Carpenter)

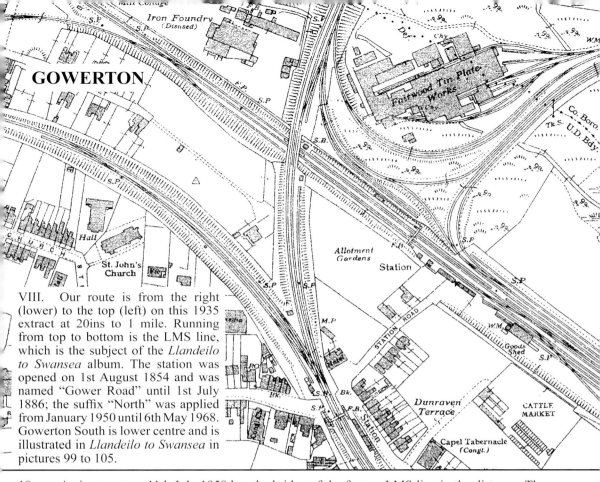

GOWERTON

VIII. Our route is from the right (lower) to the top (left) on this 1935 extract at 20ins to 1 mile. Running from top to bottom is the LMS line, which is the subject of the *Llandeilo to Swansea* album. The station was opened on 1st August 1854 and was named "Gower Road" until 1st July 1886; the suffix "North" was applied from January 1950 until 6th May 1968. Gowerton South is lower centre and is illustrated in *Llandeilo to Swansea* in pictures 99 to 105.

18.   A view west on 11th July 1958 has the bridge of the former LMS line in the distance. There were 22 men employed here in the 1930s, but staffing ceased on 28th September 1964. West Box was at the far end of the up platform between about 1882 and 1953. (H.C.Casserley)

19.　　Departing east on the same day is no. 4937 *Lanelay Hall*. In the right distance is the 1912 East Box (49 levers) which served until 12th May 1969. Beyond it had been New Gorwydd Colliery siding until about 1925. One was added for an aircraft factory in 1940, this being used by ICI from 1946 until 1964. On the right is the goods yard, which closed on 17th June 1965. (R.M.Casserley)

Gowerton	1903	1913	1923	1933
Passenger tickets issued	50593	95783	51115	25291
Season tickets issued	*	*	291	103
Parcels forwarded	3480	15938	21298	24105
General goods forwarded (tons)	1258	5331	5439	1821
Coal and coke received (tons)	16328	34566	13503	2988
Other minerals received (tons)	51071	70018	101978	109733
General goods received (tons)	4923	19050	19313	10594
Coal and Coke handled	906	17726	42426	50961
Trucks of livestock handled	37	80	267	250
* Not Available				

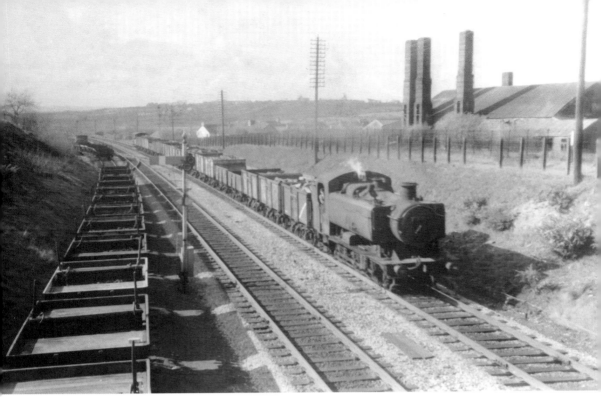

20.   This location is top left on the map and the line curving to the left served Elba Steel Works. On the right is an old foundry. Running east on 3rd August 1960 is 0-6-0PT no. 8454. The connection was lost on 22nd December 1968. (D.K.Jones coll.)

21.   There was over five miles of single track from a point just west of Cockett Tunnel. The remaining platform was on the south side and was used mainly by Shrewsbury trains. A small group wait on 25th July 2009 to witness the passing of the new steam locomotive, *Tornado*. (V.Mitchell)

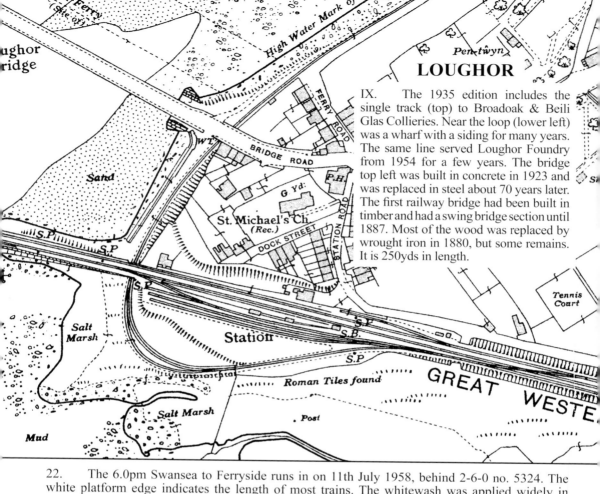

LOUGHOR

IX.   The 1935 edition includes the single track (top) to Broadoak & Beili Glas Collieries. Near the loop (lower left) was a wharf with a siding for many years. The same line served Loughor Foundry from 1954 for a few years. The bridge top left was built in concrete in 1923 and was replaced in steel about 70 years later. The first railway bridge had been built in timber and had a swing bridge section until 1887. Most of the wood was replaced by wrought iron in 1880, but some remains. It is 250yds in length.

22.   The 6.0pm Swansea to Ferryside runs in on 11th July 1958, behind 2-6-0 no. 5324. The white platform edge indicates the length of most trains. The whitewash was applied widely in World War II, due to the blackout. (H.C.Casserley)

23.   The full scene was recorded on the same day. Goods and passenger services were both withdrawn on 4th April 1960. The 1901 census showed 2543 residents; the 1961 figure was 3483. The signal box had 26 levers and was in use until 26th November 1961. (H.C.Casserley)

24.   There were just two or three men here between 1929 and 1938. This is a westward view in 1961. Further east, there had been a siding and signal box for Cae Duke Colliery from 1893 to 1933. The building became a private residence and the sidings, plus the up track, were removed later. (Stations UK)

Loughor	1903	1913	1923	1933
Passenger tickets issued	43549	65405	31197	15559
Season tickets issued	*	*	247	28
Parcels forwarded	1437	4488	2137	3017
General goods forwarded (tons)	67	80	558	25
Coal and coke received (tons)	33	1039	2927	693
Other minerals received (tons)	4098	4482	1597	1022
General goods received (tons)	332	2844	3913	4033
Coal and Coke handled	-	622	195	133
Trucks of livestock handled	6	7	1	-
* Not Available				

LLANDEILO JUNCTION

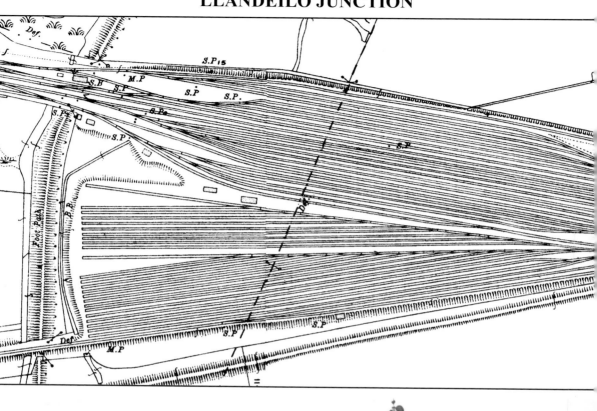

X.   This 1916 edition shows the spelling used until June 1966. Our 1852 route is from lower right to top left. Upper right to lower left is the 1839 line of the Llanelly Railway & Dock Company. The GWR ran across it on the level until 1913, although a connection was made between the two after the broad gauge was abandoned. LR&D passenger trains passed over the main line from 1850 until 1879, after which time they used the main line to and from Llanelly.

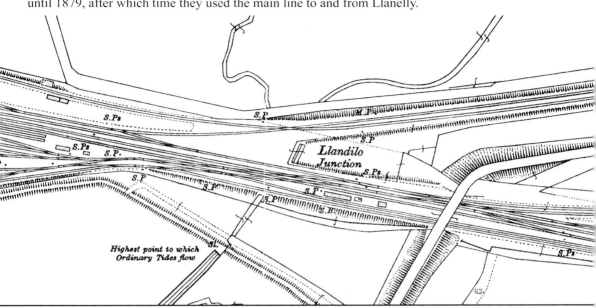

S.Ps

S.Ps   S.P.

S.P

S.P

S.P

Llandilo
Junction   S.P

S.Ps

S.P

S.P.

S.B

S.P

S.Ps

*Highest point to which
Ordinary Tides flow*

◀   25. We start with three views of the complex junction recorded on 21st September 1963. This is East Junction box, looking towards Llanelly. Its closure came on 10th December 1973, by which time it had 132 levers. (P.J.Garland/R.S.Carpenter)

26.   We move further west to look at West Junction box, again from the east. It had 68 levers. The box closed on 28th November 1966 and most of the sidings were lost between that time and 1972. (P.J.Garland/R.S.Carpenter)

27.   We go further towards Llanelly to see the up marshalling sidings. The ramp between the rails (lower right) was part of the Automatic Train Control system of the GWR. (P.J.Garland/R.S.Carpenter)

28.   No. 33014 was photographed on 16th June 1983, while hauling a train from Swansea bound for Milford Haven. The lines on the left are still used by trains on the Llandeilo route and the Swansea District Line, which bypasses Swansea and rejoins the main line at Neath. The latter was used by one DMU daily in 2009, running to and from Fishguard Harbour. (T.Heavyside)

29.   The private siding for Trostre Tinplate Works dates from 31st December 1956, but it is largely hidden by bushes. The works construction began in 1947 and production started in 1951. Fifty years later, the output was in excess of 500,000 tons annually. Most steel arrives by rail 2mm thick in coils and much coated material leaves 0.04mm thick. No. 37240 is heading east with an inspection saloon on 16th June 1983. (T.Heavyside)

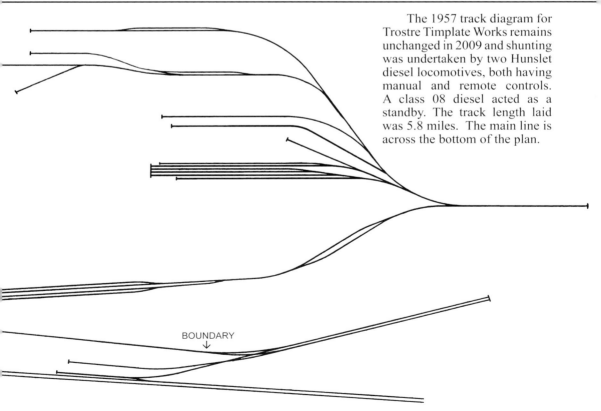

The 1957 track diagram for Trostre Timplate Works remains unchanged in 2009 and shunting was undertaken by two Hunslet diesel locomotives, both having manual and remote controls. A class 08 diesel acted as a standby. The track length laid was 5.8 miles. The main line is across the bottom of the plan.

BOUNDARY

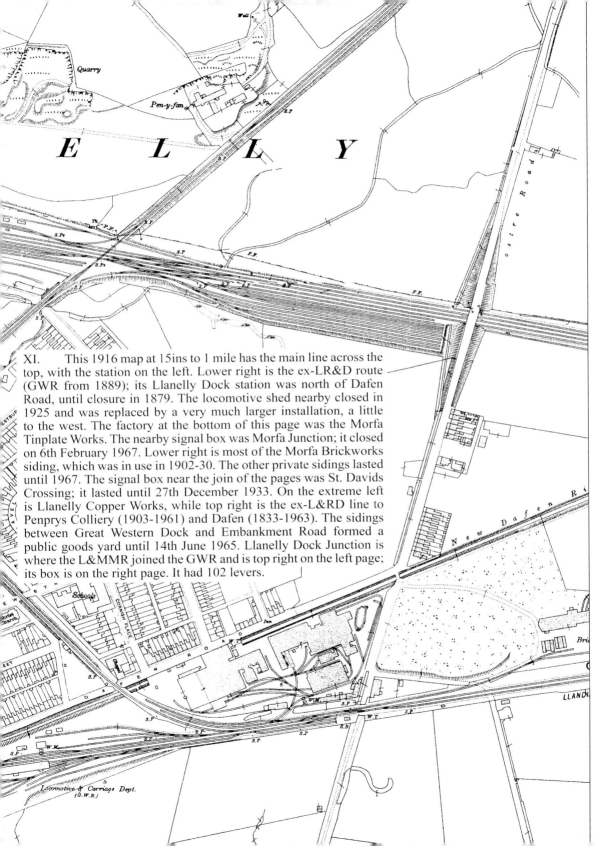

XI.   This 1916 map at 15ins to 1 mile has the main line across the top, with the station on the left. Lower right is the ex-LR&D route (GWR from 1889); its Llanelly Dock station was north of Dafen Road, until closure in 1879. The locomotive shed nearby closed in 1925 and was replaced by a very much larger installation, a little to the west. The factory at the bottom of this page was the Morfa Tinplate Works. The nearby signal box was Morfa Junction; it closed on 6th February 1967. Lower right is most of the Morfa Brickworks siding, which was in use in 1902-30. The other private sidings lasted until 1967. The signal box near the join of the pages was St. Davids Crossing; it lasted until 27th December 1933. On the extreme left is Llanelly Copper Works, while top right is the ex-L&RD line to Penprys Colliery (1903-1961) and Dafen (1833-1963). The sidings between Great Western Dock and Embankment Road formed a public goods yard until 14th June 1965. Llanelly Dock Junction is where the L&MMR joined the GWR and is top right on the left page; its box is on the right page. It had 102 levers.

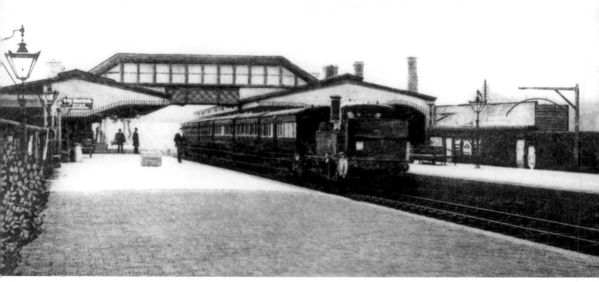

30.   A down train was recorded in about 1910, but no details exist. The loading gauge was at the end of two sidings, which lasted until 1966. A riot during a railway strike in August 1911 resulted in six fatalities nearby. (Lens of Sutton coll.)

31.   This postcard view is from the footbridge at the east end of the station which saved users of New Dock Road having to wait when the level crossing gates were closed. (SLS coll.)

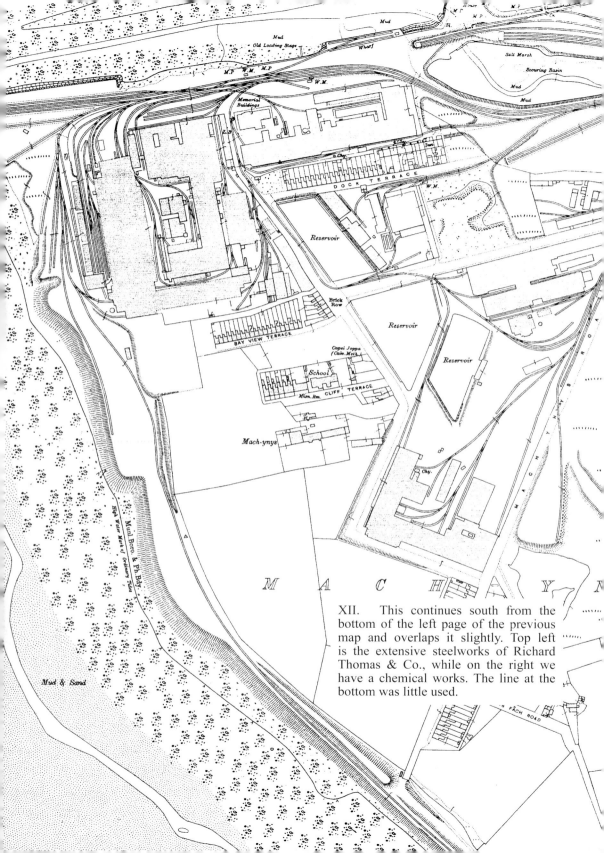

Mud

Old Loading Stage

Wharf

Mud

Salt Marsh

Scouring Basin

Mud

Mud

M.P W.M. M.P

W.M.

Memorial
Buildings

DOCK TERRACE

W.M.

Reservoir

Brick
Row

Reservoir

BAY VIEW TERRACE

Reservoir

Capel Joppa
(Calv. Meth.)

School

CLIFF TERRACE

Miss. Rm.

Mach-ynys

Chy.

High Water Mark of Ordinary Tides

Muni Boro & Ph. Bdy.

△

M   A   C   H   Y   N   Y   S   R   O   A   D

M   A   C   H   Y   N

XII. This continues south from the
bottom of the left page of the previous
map and overlaps it slightly. Top left
is the extensive steelworks of Richard
Thomas & Co., while on the right we
have a chemical works. The line at the
bottom was little used.

Mud & Sand

FACH ROAD

32. The station was rebuilt in 1877 to the form seen here in the 1930s; both footbridges are included. There were around 60 men dealing with passenger traffic in that period and just over 100 on goods matters. (Stations UK)

33. An up bay platform was provided at the east end and it is occupied by 0-6-0PT no. 8752 one day in August 1948. Signalled to depart is no. 4981 *Abberley Hall*. (Lens of Sutton coll.)

34.   Another up departure was recorded on 11th August 1960. The locomotive is no. 5908 *Moreton Hall*. The tank and its intricate tracery survived the end of steam by several years. (D.A.Johnson)

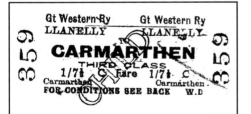

Gt Western Ry   Gt Western Ry
LLANELLY   LLANELLY
359
CARMARTHEN
THIRD CLASS
1/7½ C Fare 1/7½ C
Carmarthen   Carmarthen
FOR CONDITIONS SEE BACK   W.D

7 | 8 | 9 | 10 | 11 | 12
British Transport Commission (W)
B.R. 4406
LLANELLY (A)
PLATFORM TICKET 1d.
Available **one hour** on day of issue only.
Not valid in trains. Not transferable.
To be given up when leaving platform.
For conditions see over
1 | 2 | 3 | 4 | 5 | 6

Llanelly	1903	1913	1923	1933
Passenger tickets issued	268380	368391	385897	207891
Season tickets issued	*	*	2154	2025
Parcels forwarded	71461	132301	160526	224192
General goods forwarded (tons)	34709	154101	167546	159091
Coal and coke received (tons)	261856	421727	615053	303316
Other minerals received (tons)	112796	276042	506243	236299
General goods received (tons)	45678	124339	135852	104564
Coal and Coke handled	87267	332354	814507‡	811891‡
Trucks of livestock handled	485	613	795	135

* Not Available   ‡ Includes "Permitted" Traffic

Gt. Western Ry.   Gt. Western Ry.
Kidwelly Flats Halt Kidwelly Flats Halt
1765
TO
LLANELLY
THIRD CLASS
1/2 C Fare 1/2 C
Llanelly   Llanelly
FOR CONDITIONS SEE BACK

LLANELLI

35.   The gate wheel is included in this unusual record of no. D1058 running round a Llandrindod Wells to Plymouth excursion on 4th August 1974. The spelling of the town was changed in June 1966. The goods shed roof is in the distance; the yard had a 6-ton crane installed in 1930 and goods traffic ceased in 1965. This is East Box, which had 32 levers and closed on 12th February 1983. (R.A.Lumber/D.H.Mitchell coll.)

36.   All trains between Shrewsbury and Swansea via Llandeilo reversed here after 1964, following a period of termination here. This is the 12.25 Swansea to Shrewsbury on 26th August 1977. West Box is a white spot in the distance. It had 37 levers and was still in use as a gate box in 2009, when the station could also boast as having a buffet and ticket office. (R.F.Roberts/SLS)

37.   Improvements, including a new ticket office, came about in 1979. We witness no. 47485 arriving with a Milford Haven to Swansea train on 16th June 1983. In the background is Glanmor Road level crossing and West Box. It was downgraded on 3rd February 1969, when it became a ground frame for the gates. (T.Heavyside)

Other views of this station can be seen in pictures 99 to 105 in *Llandeilo to Swansea.*

38.   This eastward view is from August 1987. Provision was made for the down platform to accommodate two trains at once, to facilitate connections. (D.K.Jones)

SOUTH OF LLANELLY

39.   The 1925 engine shed contained two turntables 65ft long, from which the tracks radiated. This is the east end on 24th June 1962, with no. 4099 *Kilgerran Castle* out of steam. On the right is the chimney of the sand dryer. The depot was close to the bottom of the join in map XI. (J.H.Bamsey/D.H.Mitchell coll.)

40.   At rest on 22nd August 1963 is ex-BP&GVR 0-6-2T, bearing GWR no. 2168. It was built by Hudswell Clarke in 1912 and withdrawn in 1956. There were 62 locomotives allocated here in 1947. (D.T.Rowe)

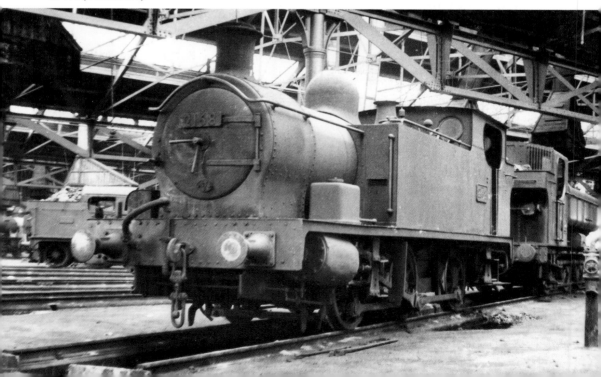

41.   The machine shop was photographed in September 1965, when everything was worked by line shafting and leather belts. Left and right are hearths for the forges. (R.M.Casserley)

42.   Power for the shafting was provided by this single cylinder steam engine in the corner. Total closure came on 1st November 1965, when the coding was 87F. The GWR code had been LLY. (R.M.Casserley)

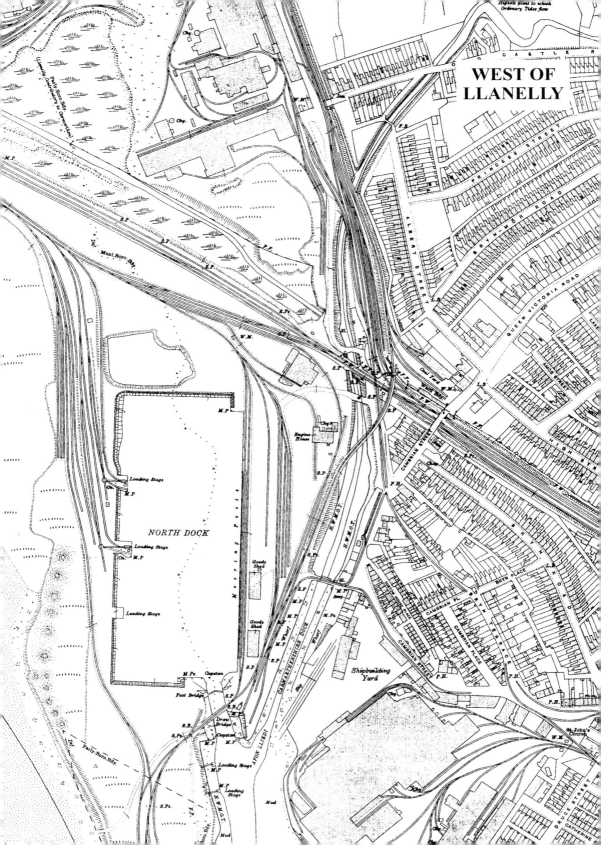

WEST OF LLANELLY

NORTH DOCK

CARMARTHENSHIRE DOCK

AFON LLIEDI

Shipbuilding Yard

Engine House

St. John's Church

PRINCESS STREET

BRYNMOR ROAD

QUEEN VICTORIA ROAD

ALBERT STREET

HIGH STREET

CAMBRIAN STREET

CAMBRIAN PLACE

DRUCE STREET

Loading Stage

Goods Shed

Mooring Posts

Foot Bridge

Draw Bridge

Capstan

XIII.   The station is lower right and this part overlaps the top left corner of map XI. The lines around North Dock were the property of the Llanelly Harbour Trust; the dock closed in 1951. At the top of the left page is the L&MMR route to Sandy Junction and to the left of it is Old Castle Tinplate Works. Near the centre of that page is Old Castle Crossing signal box (41 levers) and it was where the Stradley Estate railway crossed the main line on the level. The subsequent box closed on 12th December 1973, having been completed with 82 levers in October 1961. The line running north on the right page served a variety of premises including Marshfield Tin Works, Old Lodge Iron Works, Wern Iron Works, Llanmore Iron Works, Bres Pit, South Wales Pottery and the gasworks. The track was lifted in 1961, having earlier formed part of Nevill's Dock & Railway network. Marked "Coal Yard", this area formed Albert Road Goods Depot, which closed on 12th July 1965. It had been renamed Queen Victoria Road Depot in May 1964. The tracks in Station Road were for electric trams in 1911-33.

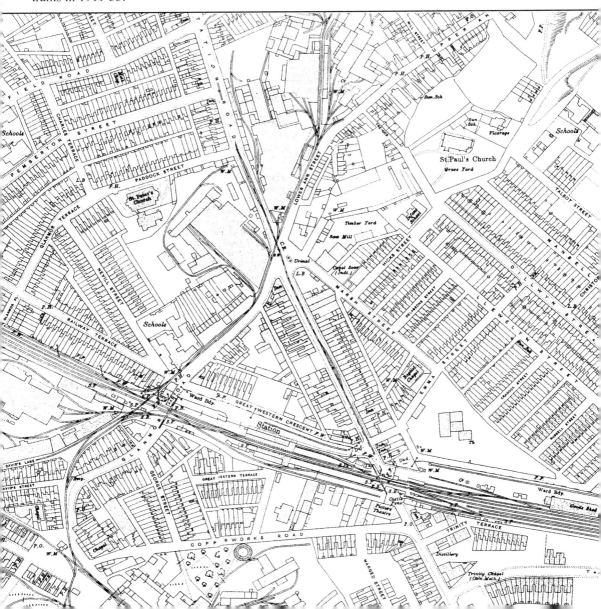

43.   The scene is Railway Terrace, in 1961; the up main line is behind the dwellings. This Peckett 0-4-0ST is one of several belonging to Nevill Druce & Co, which worked along other streets; close examination of the maps is worthwhile. (Llanelli Public Library)

44.   Between the bridge and the level crossing can be seen the single track over the main lines. It was removed in 1963. The ex-L&MMR running line to Sandy Junction is on the right; there is also one on the bridge, which runs south over the River Lleidi. We look west from Cambrian Street bridge in April 1949. Steelworks abound. (P.Copeland/Ted Hancock Books)

PEMBREY & BURRY PORT

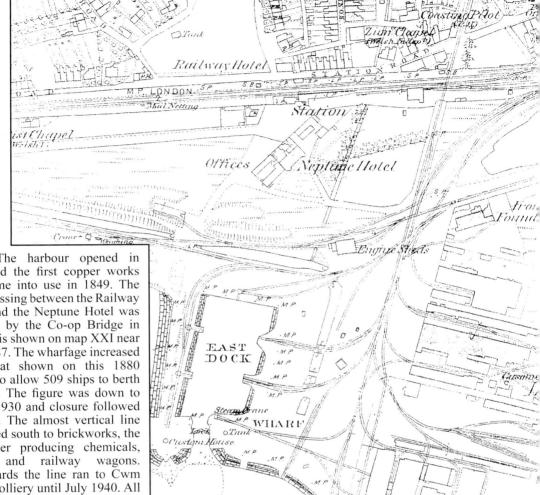

XIV. The harbour opened in 1836 and the first copper works here came into use in 1849. The level crossing between the Railway Hotel and the Neptune Hotel was replaced by the Co-op Bridge in 1893. It is shown on map XXI near picture 87. The wharfage increased from that shown on this 1880 edition to allow 509 ships to berth in 1920. The figure was down to 160 in 1930 and closure followed in 1940. The almost vertical line continued south to brickworks, the area later producing chemicals, metals and railway wagons. Northwards the line ran to Cwm Capel Colliery until July 1940. All trains were propelled, owing to the severity of the gradient. The works on the right were concerned with iron, white lead, lead and copper. One of the lines on the right (lower) eventually ran to Carmarthen Bay Power Station (see picture 96).

45.   The goods shed is in the distance, as a down train approaches in about 1910. The footbridge had been added in 1893. The wide gap between the tracks was a legacy from the broad gauge era.
(Lens of Sutton coll.)

46. A 1937 eastward view includes the goods office adjacent to the shed, which housed a crane of one ton capacity. The staff increased thus: 15 in 1903, 19 in 1913, 30 in 1923 to 58 in 1933. The suffix "and Burry Port" was added on 1st February 1887. (Stations UK)

47.   Recorded in 1958 is the south elevation. Ten years later all the land southwards was transferred from BR to the local authority. A marina was completed in 2006. The manpower dropped to 48 in 1938. (H.C.Casserley)

48.   Eastbound on 17th June 1983 is no. 37286. The signal box dated from 1906 and had been termed "East" until November 1932. The signal on the left was for the down loop. The box had been extended in 1953 to increase the frame size from 59 to 85 levers. (T.Heavyside)

49.   Recorded on the same day was the 13.00 Swansea to Milford Haven. Following the destruction of the buildings, huts were erected on the up platform; one housed a travel agency, which issued local railway tickets also. (T.Heavyside)

Pembury and Burry Port	1903	1913	1923	1933
Passenger tickets issued	85332	163933	127917	69160
Season tickets issued	*	*	1049	605
Parcels forwarded	11623	25976	25148	21456
General goods forwarded (tons)	8416	3863	14638	3708
Coal and coke received (tons)	27062	9601	35895	14912
Other minerals received (tons)	25119	11747	12694	4719
General goods received (tons)	10223	5742	8474	6392
Coal and Coke handled	4276	39499	496582‡	560475‡
Trucks of livestock handled	24	284	142	53
* Not Available ‡ Includes "Permitted" Traffic				

50.   The final view of this area features no. 08354 shunting coal on 15th June 1983. It had been brought in by one of the class 03 diesels from the Gwendraeth Valley described in pictures 87 onwards. The box continued to be used in the 21st century and was the fringe box for Port Talbot Panel. (T.Heavyside)

LANDO PLATFORM

51.   An immense Royal Ordnance Factory on the flat land near the coast and sidings, together with a halt, were provided in 1915. There was also an internal platform. The same happened in World War II. The associated signal box (42 levers) was in use from 24th July 1938 until 7th August 1966. The left signal is for the down loop, from which sidings branched in both directions. (M.Hale)

KIDWELLY FLATS HALT

52.   This was available for authorised users from about 1940 until 11th November 1957. It served the RAF Coastal Command airfield nearby. This and the previous picture date from July 1960. (M.Hale)

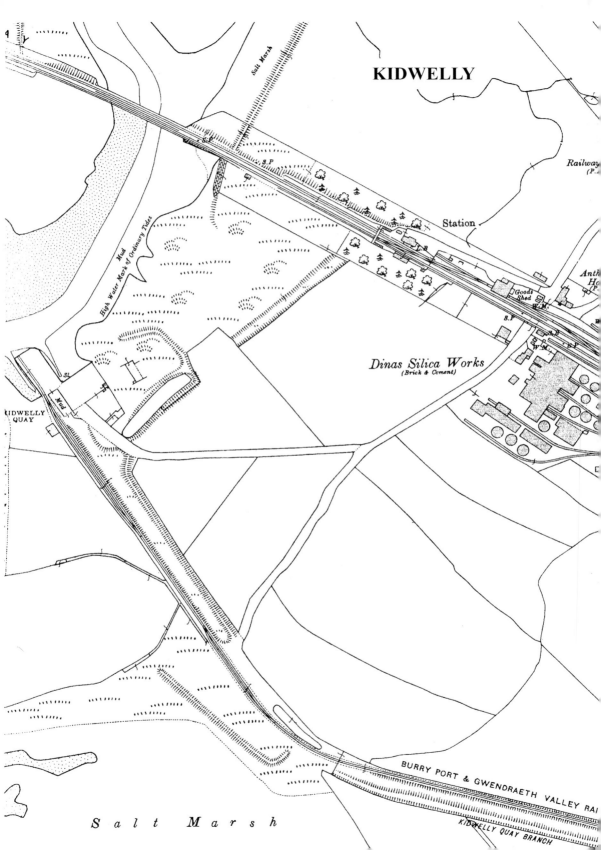

KIDWELLY

Salt Marsh

Railway
(P.

Station

Anth
Ho

Goods
Shed
W.M.

S.P

W.M.

S.P

S.P

High Water Mark of Ordinary Tides

Mud

Mud

Dinas Silica Works
(Brick & Cement)

KIDWELLY
QUAY

Sl

Mud

BURRY PORT & GWENDRAETH VALLEY RAI

KIDWELLY QUAY BRANCH

S a l t   M a r s h

XV.   The 1915 edition at 20ins to 1 mile has the GWR's main line from lower right to top left.
The upper line on the right is of the Gwendraeth Valleys Railway; the lower one is annotated and
closed on 11th October 1929.

Glan-morfa

Mountain View

Kidwelly	1903	1913	1923	1933
Passenger tickets issued	31669	41246	41244	57369
Season tickets issued	*	*	359	215
Parcels forwarded	10888	19978	17954	20117
General goods forwarded (tons)	714	10408	14316	5521
Coal and coke received (tons)	3342	10241	12778	7241
Other minerals received (tons)	777	17545	14446	9530
General goods received (tons)	5415	10733	13561	3791
Coal and Coke handled	519	6378	77905‡	11517‡
Trucks of livestock handled	153	208	115	30

* Not Available   ‡ Includes "Permitted" Traffic

W.M.
S.P

Kidwelly Junction

W.M.

Gas Works

53.　　A view southeast in the 1920s includes the crossover, but nothing of the goods yard, which is obscured by the main building (left). There were around 14 employees here in that era. (Lens of Sutton coll.)

54.　　A westward panorama on 7th July 1947 features 0-6-0PT no. 6425 with the 11.50am Carmarthen to Swansea stopping train. It has just run across the 92yd-long Kidwelly Viaduct, over the River Gwendraeth. (H.C.Casserley)

55.   The down side was recorded on the same day, but Brunel's styling had been largely lost west of Bridgend. Sadly, this building was also to be demolished. (H.C.Casserley)

56.   The siding to the gasworks closed in October 1962. The engine shed, behind the signal, had closed in 1923. The main lines are on the right, the former BP&GVR connection is to the right of the shed and the ex-GVR line is to the left of it. See the map XV for clarification. (M.Hale)

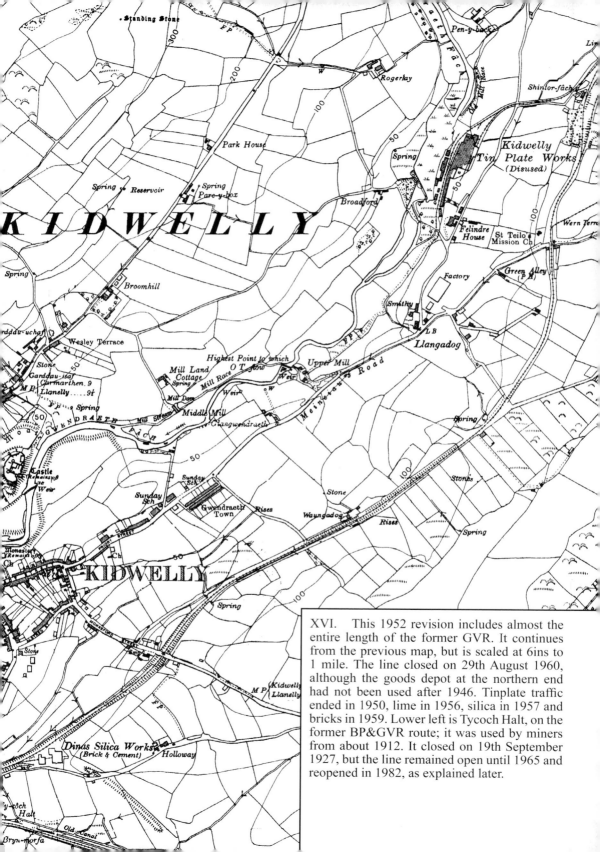

Standing Stone

FP

300

200

100

KIDWELLY

Park House

Spring
Reservoir

Spring
Parc-y-box

Broadford

50

Rogerkay

W

Pen-y-bach

Shinfor-fâch

Li

Spring

Kidwelly
Tin Plate Works
(Disused)

Felindre
House

St Teilo
Mission Ch

Wern Terr

100

Spring

Broomhill

Factory

Green Alley
(P.H.)

Smithy

LB

Llangadog

dddu-uchaf

Wesley Terrace

Stone

Garddau-isaf

Carmarthen 9

Llanelly 9¼

MP

Spring

50

FP

Spring

GWENDRAETH FACH

Mill Land
Cottage
Spring

Highest Point to which
O.T. flow

Upper Mill

Weir

Mill Race

Weir

Mill Dam

Middle Mill

Mill Stream

Grangwendraeth

W

FP

Meinciau-our Road

Spring

Castle
(Remains of)

Weir

50

50

Sunday
Sch

Sunday
Sch

Gwendraeth
Town

Rises

Stone

Waungadog

Rises

Stones

100

Spring

Monastery
(Remains of)

Ch

Ch

KIDWELLY

50

Spring

100

Stone

Smy

Kidwelly
Llanelly

MP

Dinas Silica Works
(Brick & Cement)

Holloway

FP

y-côch
Halt

Old Canal

Bryn-morfa

XVI. This 1952 revision includes almost the
entire length of the former GVR. It continues
from the previous map, but is scaled at 6ins to
1 mile. The line closed on 29th August 1960,
although the goods depot at the northern end
had not been used after 1946. Tinplate traffic
ended in 1950, lime in 1956, silica in 1957 and
bricks in 1959. Lower left is Tycoch Halt, on the
former BP&GVR route; it was used by miners
from about 1912. It closed on 19th September
1927, but the line remained open until 1965 and
reopened in 1982, as explained later.

57.   Full lifting barriers came into use in September 1978 and on 17th September 1983 the lever frame was removed, to be replaced by a panel to control the reopened junction. The photograph is from 7th August 1987. The brickwork was from the 1880s and the upper part was rebuilt in the 1960s. (D.K.Jones)

58.   Part of the goods shed and the stark new buildings were recorded on the same day, when the broad track spacing was still evident. Most trains still called, although goods traffic had ceased back in March 1964. (D.K.Jones)

SOUTH OF FERRYSIDE

59.	Splendid vistas across the estuary can be enjoyed for the remainder of the journey. The river is in the background as no. 47157 runs south with a Gulf Oil train from Milford Haven on 17th June 1983. (T.Heavyside)

➔	60. Two days earlier, a Milford Haven to Swansea train of BR Mk. I coaches was hauled by no. 33046, complete with snow ploughs. Such precipitation is unusual here. (T.Heavyside)

➔	61. Running north through drizzle on 19th September 1987 is no. 6000 King George V with the "Carmarthen Express" special from Swansea. The condition of the waterfront varies greatly in this area, with parts having a substantial sea wall. (H.Ballantyne)

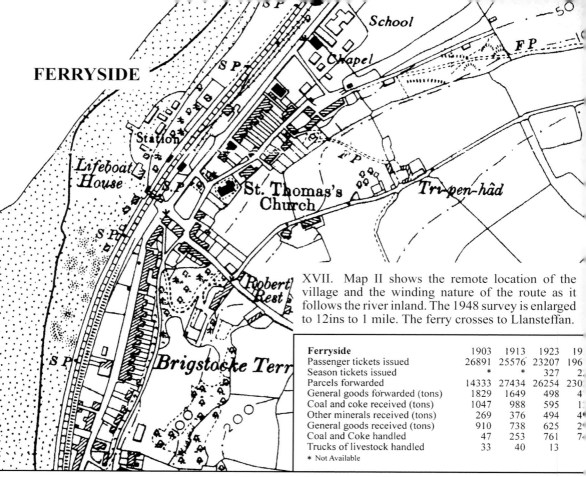

FERRYSIDE

Station

Lifeboat House

School

Chapel

S.P.

St. Thomas's Church

Tri-pen-hâd

Robert Rest

Brigstocke Terr

XVII. Map II shows the remote location of the village and the winding nature of the route as it follows the river inland. The 1948 survey is enlarged to 12ins to 1 mile. The ferry crosses to Llansteffan.

Ferryside	1903	1913	1923	19
Passenger tickets issued	26891	25576	23207	196
Season tickets issued	*	*	327	2.
Parcels forwarded	14333	27434	26254	230
General goods forwarded (tons)	1829	1649	498	4
Coal and coke received (tons)	1047	988	595	1
Other minerals received (tons)	269	376	494	4
General goods received (tons)	910	738	625	2
Coal and Coke handled	47	253	761	7
Trucks of livestock handled	33	40	13	
* Not Available				

62. The two styles of Brunel's chalet buildings can be compared in this panorama from the footbridge on 11th April 1955. A staff of six was provided in the 1930s. The parcels shed is on the right and the goods shed is in the background. The latter housed a 30cwt crane. (H.C.Casserley)

63. The same view in August 1977 shows that one siding was retained, although goods traffic had ended here on 23rd March 1964. Staffing ceased on 28th September of that year. (SLS)

64. Official vandalism in an era of ignorance resulted in two brick sheds being provided. The depressing scene is compounded by heavy rain, as no. 47560 *Tamar* heads the 11.00 Milford Haven to Swansea on 21st September 1985. (P.Jones)

65. The umbrellas are out as no. 7029 *Clun Castle* hurries through with the second steam excursion since the 1960s from Swansea to Carmarthen. The date is 19th September 1987. Lifting barriers were installed in August 1977 and the box was still in use in 2009 with 24 levers. (H.Ballantyne)

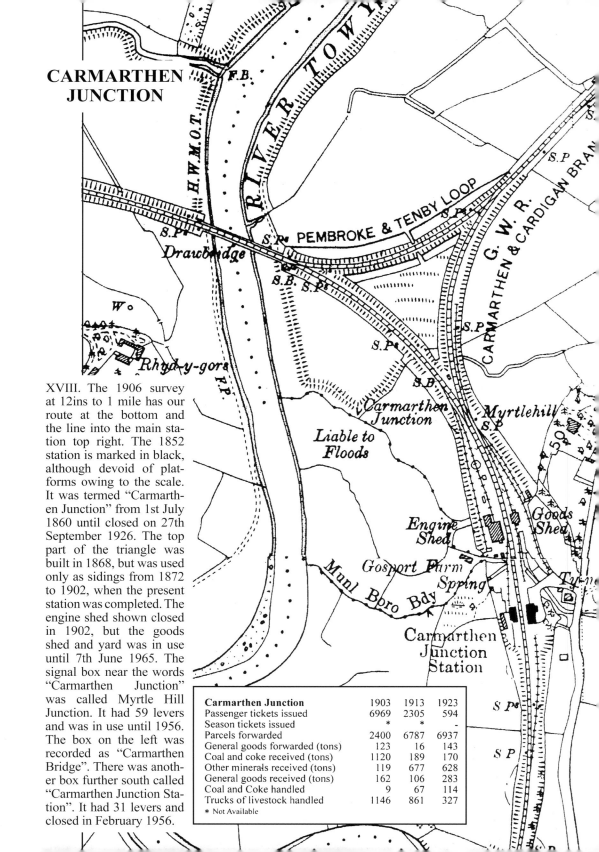

CARMARTHEN JUNCTION

XVIII. The 1906 survey at 12ins to 1 mile has our route at the bottom and the line into the main station top right. The 1852 station is marked in black, although devoid of platforms owing to the scale. It was termed "Carmarthen Junction" from 1st July 1860 until closed on 27th September 1926. The top part of the triangle was built in 1868, but was used only as sidings from 1872 to 1902, when the present station was completed. The engine shed shown closed in 1902, but the goods shed and yard was in use until 7th June 1965. The signal box near the words "Carmarthen Junction" was called Myrtle Hill Junction. It had 59 levers and was in use until 1956. The box on the left was recorded as "Carmarthen Bridge". There was another box further south called "Carmarthen Junction Station". It had 31 levers and closed in February 1956.

Carmarthen Junction	1903	1913	1923
Passenger tickets issued	6969	2305	594
Season tickets issued	*	*	-
Parcels forwarded	2400	6787	6937
General goods forwarded (tons)	123	16	143
Coal and coke received (tons)	1120	189	170
Other minerals received (tons)	119	677	628
General goods received (tons)	162	106	283
Coal and Coke handled	9	67	114
Trucks of livestock handled	1146	861	327
* Not Available			

66.   This indifferent northward view is the only one known of this location. There was a staff of 50 listed in 1913; the figure was 47 throughout the 1930s, these presumably being in the traffic department. (Lens of Sutton coll.)

67.   No. 33030 is working the 08.45 Swansea to Milford Haven on 17th June 1983 and is on the eastern curve. In the background is the avoiding line, then used mostly by oil trains and a few boat trains. (T.Heavyside)

68.   Nearing the northern apex of the triangle in 1984, we pass under the new bypass and approach the station. A new signal box was opened at the southern junction on 5th February 1956. The design was the same as used at Kidderminster and the box was still in use in 2009. Its 78-lever frame was replaced by a panel on 9th February 1985. (Ted Hancock Books)

CARMARTHEN

Ch.

Priory
Foundry

Priory Foundry

WAUN·DEW

MYRDIN

FP

WATERLOO

Gatewa
(Site of)
Chapel
(Site of)

Chap.

Chap. Priory
(Site of)

PRIORY

PRIORY STR.

Chap.

P.H.

Chap.

Ch. Sch.

NORTH PARADE

AVENUE

EAST PARADE

S.Ps

S.P

Chap.

Sch.

FRANCIS TERRACE

DUTCH PLACE

JOHN STREET

CAMBRIAN

Chap.

Sch.

KING STREET

PETERS ST.

Ch.

CHURCH ST.

Vic.

College

THE PARADE

S.P

S.P

Goods
Shed

S.P

QUEEN ST.

SPILMAN STREET

LAMMAS

Hotel

FRIARS RD

M.P

Inn

M.P

Kiln

Slip

CHAPEL RD

BLUE STREET

HALL ST.

BRIDGE STREET

CASTLE

LITT

S.P

S.P

Sun. Sch.

QUAY

Mnl. Boro.

R I

Carmarthen
Bridge

Saw Mill

S.P

S.P
S.B.

FP

Station

S.P

S.P

S.B

S.Ps

S.P

ROMAN ROAD

SARN

Sout

Sou
Vi

-mo
tage

XIX. This map continues from the top of the previous one and has the new station and incomplete locomotive depot lower left. The former opened on 1st July 1902 and the latter on 11th February 1907. The earlier station was in Station Road, north of the river until demolished in 1902. Its goods depot and engine shed are still shown. The route from Llandeilo opened in 1864 and had three different owners before the LNWR in 1891. This branch is included in the *Llandeilo to Swansea* album and closed in 1963. The signal box top right was called Carmarthen Goods Yard and it closed on 13th July 1967. The yard predeceased it. The LMS engine shed closed on 4th July 1938 and this edition includes road alterations up to that time.

P

Parc-yr-eithin

Spring

Intrenchment

New-

Pen-sarn

FP

69.   This northward view is of the GWR station soon after its completion in 1902. The suffix "Town" was transferred from the LNWR station at that time, but was not used officially. The staff number averaged 68 in the 1930s. In the distance is Crossing Box, which closed on 15th December 1968; it had a 58-lever frame. (Lens of Sutton coll.)

70.   The six-road running shed, the turntable and the coaling facilities were photographed soon after completion. One example of the latter survives at the Didcot Railway Centre. The approach gradient was 1 in 35. (GWR)

71.   The town's population rose from about 10,000 in 1901 to 13,000 in 1961. The island platform lengthening was photographed on 31st January 1931, as a 2-6-2T runs round its train. The Dean Goods 0-6-0 has probably just arrived from Aberystwyth. (GWR)

72.   We can now enjoy three photographs from 13th July 1956. At the north end is 2-6-2T no. 5558 and the girders of the bridge over the River Towy are in the distance. It carried a single track. The route north opened in 1860, closed to passengers in 1965 and to freight in 1973. (H.C.Casserley)

73. At the south end is 0-6-0PT no. 9666 and in the background is Station Box, which had 80 levers and closed on 7th May 1972. The lofty fitting shop is on the left. (H.C.Casserley)

74. No. 6903 *Belmont Hall* is standing on the through road with the 6.50pm from Neyland, prior to attaching the coaches to sleeping cars, which would depart at 8.31; arrival at Paddington would be 4.25am, via Gloucester. (H.C.Casserley)

75.   The shed allocation at the end of 1947 was 49 locomotives, plus two diesel railcars, nos 13 and 15. On the left is the fitting shop, which had a massive 30-ton capacity rope driven travelling crane. The shed closed in April 1964, when it was coded 87G. (R.M.Casserley)

76.   An atmospheric scene was recorded with good film on 16th June 1960, with the track in terminal decline. Visible on the left is no. 4923 *Evenley Hall*, together with no. 7829 *Ramsbury Manor*, 2-6-2T no. 8102 and no. 7016 *Chester Castle*. (G.Adams/M.J.Stretton coll.)

↓ 77.   Platform no. 1 is occupied by an 0-6-0PT, no. 2 by 2-6-0 no. 6316, no. 3 by a DMU and no. 4 is vacant; it was often used by the infrequent Aberystwyth service. The private siding on the left was used by milk tankers from July 1929. (G.Adams/M.J.Stretton coll.)

78.   The original 55ft turntable was replaced by this 65ft one in 1931 and was recorded on 27th August 1963. No. 4983 *Albert Hall* carries the shedplate 87H, which meant Neyland or a sub depot thereof. (D.A.Johnson)

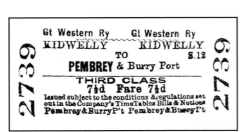

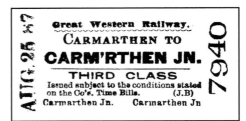

Carmarthen Town	1903	1913	1923	1933
Passenger tickets issued	105457	115981	124464	67353
Season tickets issued	*	*	350	219
Parcels forwarded	45687	69749	126657	245411
General goods forwarded (tons)	11831	13118	3583	3976
Coal and coke received (tons)	9352	10300	3751	6350
Other minerals received (tons)	3645	5781	5667	12777
General goods received (tons)	15254	20015	26697	34405
Coal and Coke handled	1386	1151	9466	12115
Trucks of livestock handled	147	777	2003	1078
* Not Available				

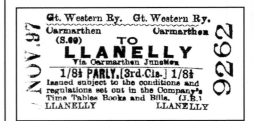

79.   Rain spoilt the record of the surroundings on 23rd September 1979, as no. 37188 waited to depart at 10.45 for Swansea. Brutes abound. (T.Heavyside)

80.   No. 47515 departs on 17th June 1983, with the 08.27 Milford Haven to Swansea, while the inbound locomotive creeps along the platform. Station Box had stood on the left until eleven years earlier. (T.Heavyside)

81.   Private sidings on the left have included ones for Aberthaw Cement and UK Fertilisers, as well as the dairy. The goods yard had a 6-ton crane. Platforms 1 and 4 had long gone when this photograph was taken on 28th April 1984. No. 2 was used by a few trains each day, although the footbridge had been removed. Nos 37180 and 37189 are running round a railtour. (D.H.Mitchell)

82.   The west elevation of the 1902 buildings was recorded in July 1987. They were little changed more than 20 years later; even the platform canopy was intact. (D.K.Jones)

2. Llanelly & Mynydd Mawr Railway

XX. The origin of the line can be traced back to 1803. The route is shown with dashes on the right and the main collieries are marked. A public passenger service was never operated, but the company had eight bogie coaches, ex-Metropolitan Railway, for the conveyance of miners. The map is reproduced from *Colonel Stephens - the Man and his Empire* (Middleton Press).

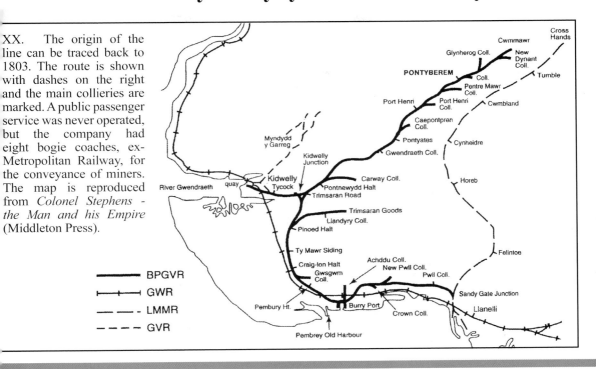

BPGVR
GWR
LMMR
GVR

SANDY JUNCTION

83.   At the eastern end of the former BP&GVR network on 26th July 1960 is ex-GWR 0-6-0PT no. 1666. The signal box was open until 25th February 1968. The location is lower right on the map. (M.Hale)

CYNHEIDRE COLLIERY

(top) 84. The date is 29th July 1966 and this is a very late steaming of an ex-GWR locomotive. It is 0-6-0PT no. 1607. Work had started on the new pit in March 1954, but it was to be November 1960 before it opened. (M.Hale)

85. This layout was completed in March 1960 and is seen in June 1983 from the site of the signal box, which was in use from 1960 to 1968. No. 37251 is in charge and the pit is on the right. It closed completely on 24th March 1989. A new L&MMR was formed in 2009 and track was obtained from Llandarcy for laying on this site. It was claimed to be the newest railway on the oldest trackbed. (T.Heavyside)

CROSS HANDS

86.   The line opened in 1883 and north of Cynheidre it served pits at Llannon (until 1922), Cae Glas (until 1926) and Great Mountain (until 1965). There were goods sidings at Tumble (until 1963) and Cwmblawd (until 1959). The line north of Tumble closed on 21st November 1966 and south thereof was sold to the National Coal Board in 1970. Cross Hands Colliery opened in 1900 and is seen on an indifferent postcard. The goods depot here closed on 25th January 1965. (A.Dudman coll.)

3. Burry Port & Gwendraeth Valley Railway
BURRY PORT

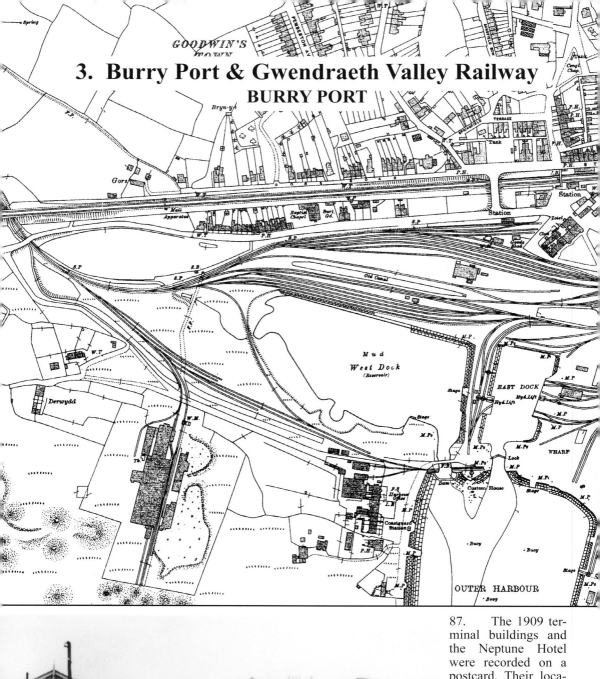

87. The 1909 terminal buildings and the Neptune Hotel were recorded on a postcard. Their location can be seen to the left of the join in the map. The lightweight flat bottom rail is evident here and elsewhere.
(Lens of Sutton coll.)

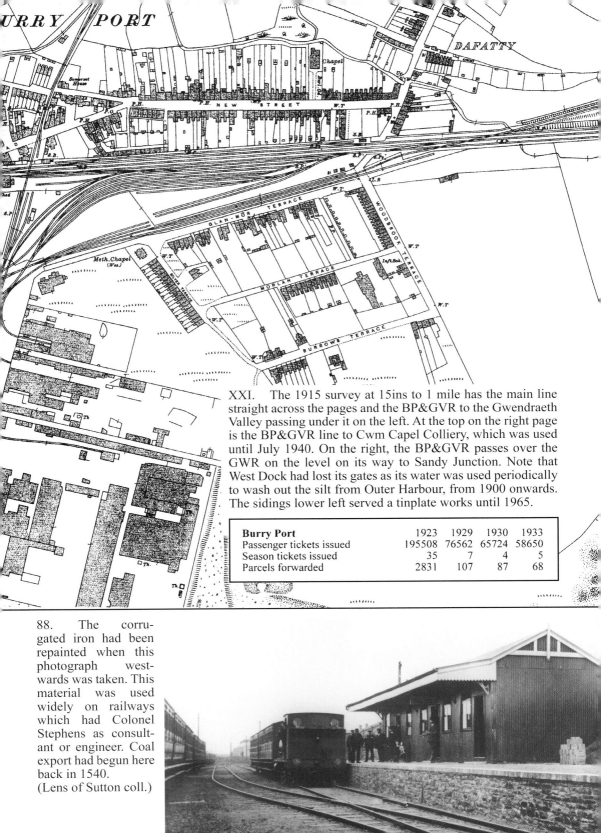

URRY PORT

DAFATTY

XXI. The 1915 survey at 15ins to 1 mile has the main line straight across the pages and the BP&GVR to the Gwendraeth Valley passing under it on the left. At the top on the right page is the BP&GVR line to Cwm Capel Colliery, which was used until July 1940. On the right, the BP&GVR passes over the GWR on the level on its way to Sandy Junction. Note that West Dock had lost its gates as its water was used periodically to wash out the silt from Outer Harbour, from 1900 onwards. The sidings lower left served a tinplate works until 1965.

Burry Port	1923	1929	1930	1933
Passenger tickets issued	195508	76562	65724	58650
Season tickets issued	35	7	4	5
Parcels forwarded	2831	107	87	68

88. The corrugated iron had been repainted when this photograph westwards was taken. This material was used widely on railways which had Colonel Stephens as consultant or engineer. Coal export had begun here back in 1540.
(Lens of Sutton coll.)

89.　　No. 1967 is waiting to leave for Cwmmawr at 1.45pm on 7th July 1947. The train has two four-wheeled coaches and two bogies. It would return in two parts. The area had been created as a New Town in 1850. (H.C.Casserley)

90.　　We look west across the join in the map, at the engine sheds in September 1962, as a class 03 diesel undertakes shunting. The sheds had closed in February 1962 and steam operation of the branch ceased on 4th October 1965. Motive power came from Llanelli shed during that period. (R.S.Carpenter)

91.   A view in the other direction at the west end of the yard has the Neptune Hotel in the right background and the starting signal near the signal box. The date is 16th May 1964. (P.J.Garland/R.S.Carpenter)

92.   The west elevations of the engine sheds were photographed on the same day, along with the coal stage, to the left of them. The road across the sidings offered a dangerous link between Neptune Square and the docks. The shed code was BP in the GWR era; it was sub to 87F thereafter. (P.J.Garland/R.S.Carpenter)

93. An SLS special is about to leave the sidings on 16th May 1964, hauled by 0-6-0ST no. 1665. The same road is evident again. The engine sheds were demolished in 1990. There had been an allocation of eleven tank engines back in 1947. (G.Adams/M.J.Stretton coll.)

94. The signalman was pictured from the leading van on the return journey. The box had been built in 1959 with four levers, but was closed on 27th June 1965. The first box was erected here in 1909 and it had only three levers. (P.J.Garland/R.S.Carpenter)

95.   The passenger station was intact ten years after the last ticket had been issued, but the buffer stop was beyond further use. (Stations UK)

96.   The afternoon train of anthracite to Coedbach Washery is about to pass under the main line on 7th September 1983, hauled by nos 03119 and 03141, with no. 03152 at the rear. In the background is Carmarthen Bay Power Station, which had its own sidings when generating in 1953-83. The Neptune Hotel stands out in white and on the right is Marcroft Wagon Works, which opened in 1977. Owing to the origin of the route being a canal, there were many low bridges, which meant these locomotives had to have their cab roofs lowered. The line was subject to flooding under bridges. (H.Ballantyne)

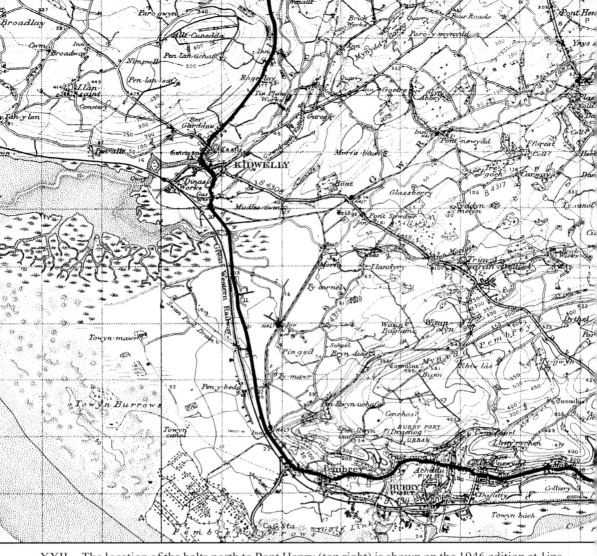

XXII.   The location of the halts north to Pont Henry (top right) is shown on the 1946 edition at 1 ins to 1 mile. Both Burry Port stations are at the bottom. The extensive sidings and buildings to the left are part of Lando Royal Ordnance Factory, but are not annotated as such for security resons.

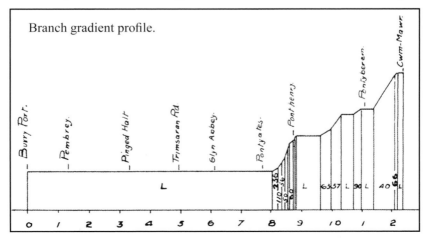

Branch gradient profile.

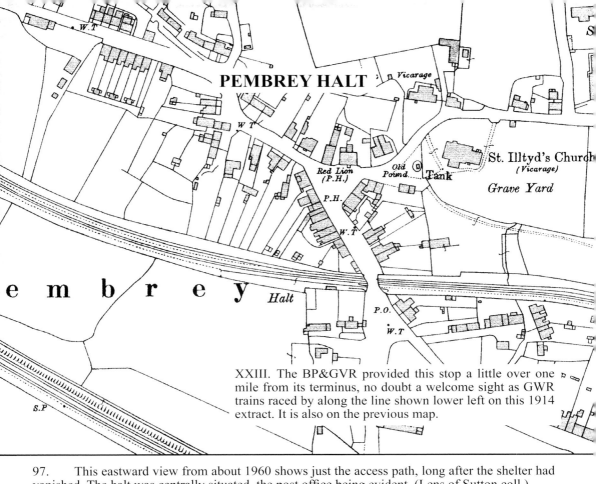

PEMBREY HALT

Vicarage

Red Lion
(P.H.)

Old
Pound

Tank

St. Illtyd's Church
(Vicarage)

Grave Yard

P.H.

W.T

e m b r e y Halt

P.O.

W.T

S.P

XXIII. The BP&GVR provided this stop a little over one
mile from its terminus, no doubt a welcome sight as GWR
trains raced by along the line shown lower left on this 1914
extract. It is also on the previous map.

97.   This eastward view from about 1960 shows just the access path, long after the shelter had
vanished. The halt was centrally situated, the post office being evident. (Lens of Sutton coll.)

CRAIGLON BRIDGE HALT

98.   This platform did not come into use until 1st February 1932 and was on the west side of the line. South of it was Carreg Llwyd Quarries, which had sidings on the east side from 1926 until sometime in the 1950s. (Lens of Sutton coll.)

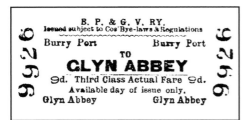

B. P. & G. V. RY.
Issued subject to Co's Bye-laws & Regulations
Burry Port   Burry Port
TO
GLYN ABBEY
9d. Third Class Actual Fare 9d.
Available day of issue only.
Glyn Abbey   Glyn Abbey
9926   9926

B. P. & G. V. RY.
Issued subject to Co's Bye-laws & Regulations
Trimsaran Rd.   Trimsaran Rd.
TO
PONTYBEREM
6d. THIRD CLASS 6d.
Available day of issue only.
Pontyberem   Pontyberem
9172   9172

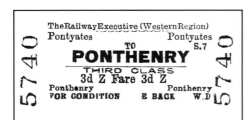

The Railway Executive (Western Region)
Pontyates   Pontyates
TO   S.7
PONTHENRY
THIRD CLASS
3d Z Fare 3d Z
Ponthenry   Ponthenry
FOR CONDITION   E BACK   W.D
5740   5740

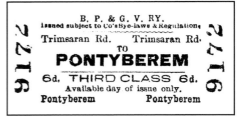

Gt. Western Ry.   Gt. Western Ry
Pontyberem   Pontyberem
TO
CWMMAWR
THIRD CLASS
5½d Z Fare 5½d Z
Cwmmawr   Cwmmawr
FOR CONDITIONS SEE BACK   C.L
8818   8818

PINGED HALT

Morfa-isaf

Pony Halt *Plough* *(P B)*

Ford *F B* *Rises*

Fords

Ty-wrth-y-morfa-uchaf

Ty-wrth-y-morfa-isaf

P E M B R E Y

Kidwelly Flats Station

Ty-gwyn

Saltrock Farm

Clôs

Tŷ-maw

XXIV. The 1948 edition at 6ins to 1 mile has the main line on the left, together with Kidwelly Flats Halt. It was an unadvertised stop between about 1940 and 1957 for the RAF. The branch is to the right and the earthworks, between the two routes, represent the alignment of the pre-railway canal. The halt is top right.

Pen-y-bedd

F B

M P

M P
Kidwelly...8
Llanelly..6½

Old Canal

99. The overgrown canal is on the right of this 1964 record of the remnants of the halt, looking north. In 1951, the population of Pinged (usual PIN-GED, with a hard G) was 80. The boundary between the ground was subjected to track weedkiller and that, influenced by residual canal water, created a unique environment for the rare Prostrate Toadflax. (Stations UK)

TRIMSARAN ROAD

100. We look under Trimsaran Road towards Kidwelly Junction in about 1960. The outer tracks were running lines and the centre two acted as exchange sidings. The remains of the platform are on the left. (Lens of Sutton coll.)

XXV. The 1948 survey at 6ins to 1 mile has the line from Pinged Halt lower left and Trimsaran Road Halt at the top of the left page. To the left of it is Kidwelly Junction signal box, which was in use from 1909 until 1967, when the Kidwelly Loop was abandoned. Coedbach Disposal Centre was established near the left ↘

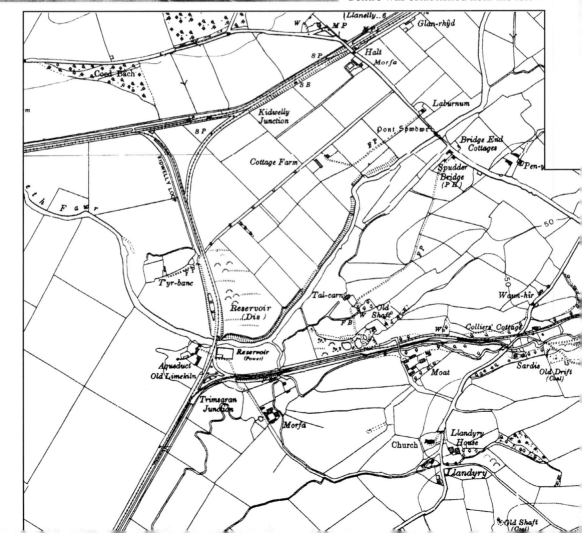

border of the map in 1956, but the link to Kidwelly was lost between 1965 and 1983. The Trimsaran branch runs across the pages, but it never carried passengers. There was however a public goods depot in the village until 1964, when the colliery and also the branch closed. Traffic had begun on 16th October 1872 and continued east for almost a mile to a brickworks for many years.

101.   The platform was more evident when viewed from the B4038 bridge in 1964. The signals were removed in 1967. The population of Trimsaran was 200 in 1951. (Stations UK)

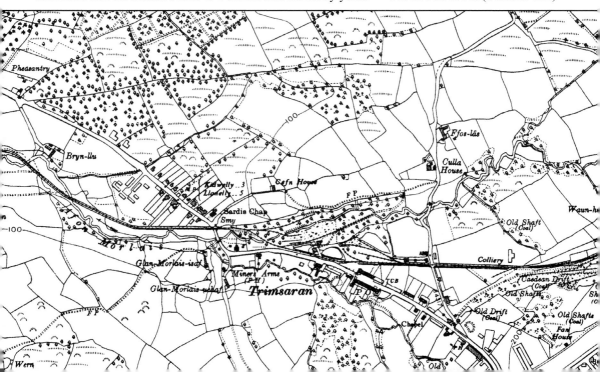

COEDBACH WASHERY

102.   The train in picture no. 96 is seen again, heading towards Cwmmawr on 7th September 1983. The washery would be on a through route within weeks. (H.Ballantyne)

103.   The original BP&GVR route to Kidwelly was closed in 1965. This is the reopening special on 27th October 1983, hauled by no. 37180 *Sir Dyfed/County of Dyfed*; the coaches were for invited guests. The link restoration brought an end to the branch height restriction and larger wagons could be used. (NCB)

↓   104.   Shunting on 10th January 1989 is no. 08994 *Gwendraeth*, in Railfreight livery. Its height had earlier been reduced for use on the branch. Several others were subject to such surgery. (H.Ballantyne)

GLYN ABBEY HALT

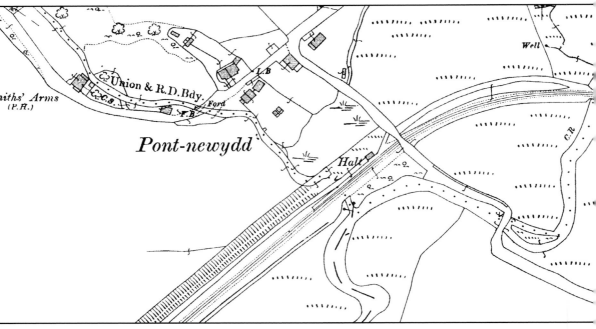

XXVI.   Until about November 1911, the halt was called Pontnewydd, the nearest community on this 1915 map. Glyn Abbey was larger; its population had reached 150 by 1951.

105.   A southbound two-coach train was recorded shortly before cessation of passenger service in 1953, when the shelter was still standing. Southwest of the halt was Carway Siding, on the east side of the line. It was laid on the route of a former canal branch and was almost ¼ mile in length. (Lens of Sutton coll.)

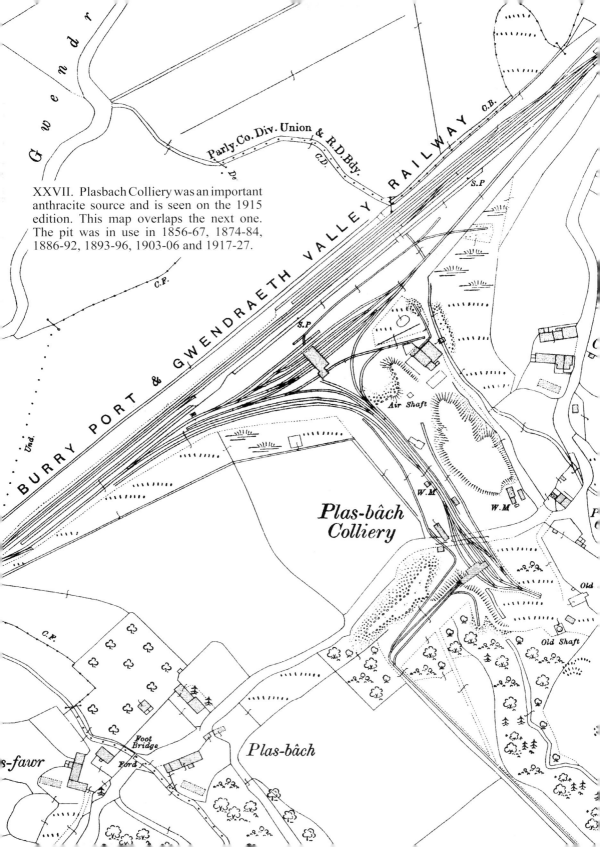

XXVII. Plasbach Colliery was an important anthracite source and is seen on the 1915 edition. This map overlaps the next one. The pit was in use in 1856-67, 1874-84, 1886-92, 1893-96, 1903-06 and 1917-27.

PONTYATES

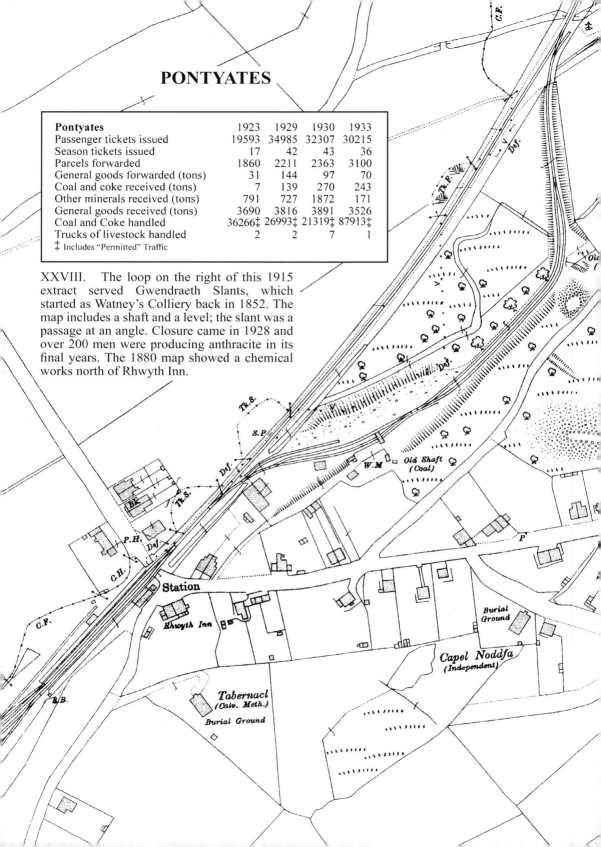

Pontyates	1923	1929	1930	1933
Passenger tickets issued	19593	34985	32307	30215
Season tickets issued	17	42	43	36
Parcels forwarded	1860	2211	2363	3100
General goods forwarded (tons)	31	144	97	70
Coal and coke received (tons)	7	139	270	243
Other minerals received (tons)	791	727	1872	171
General goods received (tons)	3690	3816	3891	3526
Coal and Coke handled	36266‡	26993‡	21319‡	87913‡
Trucks of livestock handled	2	2	7	1
‡ Includes "Permitted" Traffic				

XXVIII.   The loop on the right of this 1915 extract served Gwendraeth Slants, which started as Watney's Colliery back in 1852. The map includes a shaft and a level; the slant was a passage at an angle. Closure came in 1928 and over 200 men were producing anthracite in its final years. The 1880 map showed a chemical works north of Rhwyth Inn.

106.   The colliery tip is in the background in this northward postcard view. South of the station, trains used the 1836 stone canal aqueduct to pass over the waters of the Gwendraeth Fawr, until it was rebuilt in steel in 1917. (Lens of Sutton coll.)

107.   A panorama in the same direction in 1958 reveals widespread neglect, but also the position of the water column, the lamp hut and the gents. There were 2000 living nearby in 1951 and ten employees here in the 1930s. (R.M.Casserley)

108.   A closer view of the urinal reveals the unusually high location of the obligatory fire buckets and a rare example of partial roofing. We see iron sheeting on the left and cast iron on the right. (R.M.Casserley)

109.   The signal box (right) was in use from 1909 to 1962 and the goods yard (left) closed on 12th July 1965. This picture is from 1964. The box initially had eight levers, but this was increased to 14 in about 1913. The line on the right was not used after January 1964. (Stations UK)

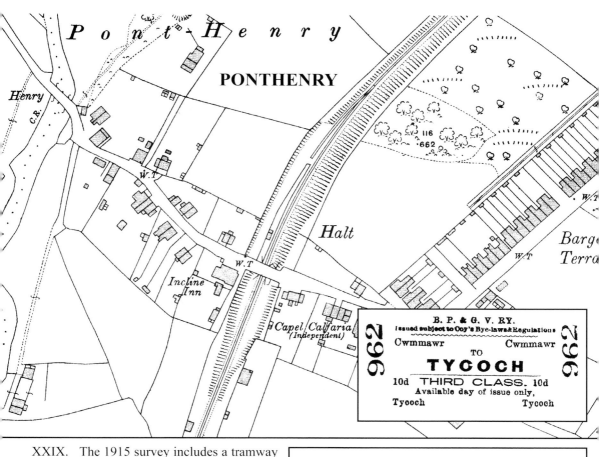

B. P. & G. V. RY.
Issued subject to Coy's Bye-laws & Regulations

Cwmmawr   Cwmmawr
TO
TYCOCH
10d   THIRD CLASS. 10d
Available day of issue only,
Tyooch   Tyooch

XXIX. The 1915 survey includes a tramway track from Ponthenry Colliery running close to the private coal sheds of Bargoed Terrace.

110. The map shows part of a platform on the outside of the curve, the position it occupied until about 1920. The remains of the brick-built station are seen in 1958. The steepest part of the climb was a little to the south and was at 1 in 45 - the siding is level. (R.M.Casserley)

Ponthenry	1923	1929	1930	1933
Passenger tickets issued	10769	13986	14266	16209
Season tickets issued	2	27	22	36
Parcels forwarded	1085	1226	1294	1749
General goods forwarded (tons)	45	21	29	23
Coal and coke received (tons)	-	49	277	74
Other minerals received (tons)	522	306	62	18
General goods received (tons)	1428	3486	3748	2969
Coal and Coke handled	48599‡	41573‡	44930‡	32107‡
Trucks of livestock handled	2	-	-	-

‡ Includes "Permitted" Traffic

PONTYBEREM

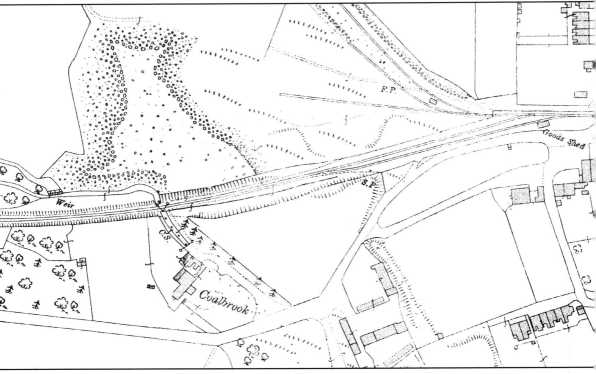

XXX. The 1915 survey shows the goods shed remote from the station, which it predated. There was another goods siding further west, this having a cart weighing machine.

111. A saddle tank with a train from Burry Port arrives within the first four years of the life of the station, when it was a terminus. A staff of four was listed in 1923-38. (Lens of Sutton coll.)

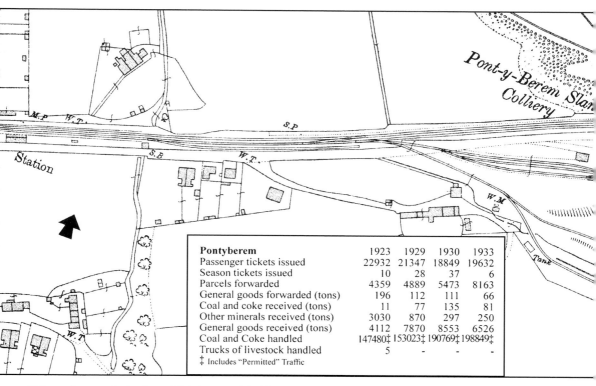

Pontyberem	1923	1929	1930	1933
Passenger tickets issued	22932	21347	18849	19632
Season tickets issued	10	28	37	6
Parcels forwarded	4359	4889	5473	8163
General goods forwarded (tons)	196	112	111	66
Coal and coke received (tons)	11	77	135	81
Other minerals received (tons)	3030	870	297	250
General goods received (tons)	4112	7870	8553	6526
Coal and Coke handled	147480‡	153023‡	190769‡	198849‡
Trucks of livestock handled	5	-	-	-
‡ Includes "Permitted" Traffic				

112.   A second platform (right) was added in 1913, when passenger services were extended east to Cwmmawr. The 13-lever signal box (left) and the loop were provided at that time. This picture dates from July 1958. (H.C.Casserley)

113.   This is the driver's view of the goods shed in 1964. It would close the following year. Its siding had become a loop in 1911. There were around 3500 residents in 1951.
(P.J.Garland/R.S.Carpenter)

114.   The train seen in earlier pictures is passing the site of the station on 7th September 1983, bound for Cwmmawr with anthracite after washing at Coedbach. (H.Ballantyne)

➔ XXXI.   There were 2250 folk living nearby in 1951. The station opened in 1913 and this survey was two years later. The sidings for New Dynant Colliery were in use from 1905 until pit closure in 1939. It had its own 0-4-0ST, *Edith*. The sidings at the top were for Closyryn Colliery, which closed in 1925, but reopened briefly around 1931.

↘ 115. First we have two views from 7th July 1947. On the right is 0-6-0PT no. 1967 waiting to leave with the 3.20pm to Burry Port, while no. 1957 stands on the left with the 4.15. Both have two coaches. (H.C.Casserley)

CWMMAWR

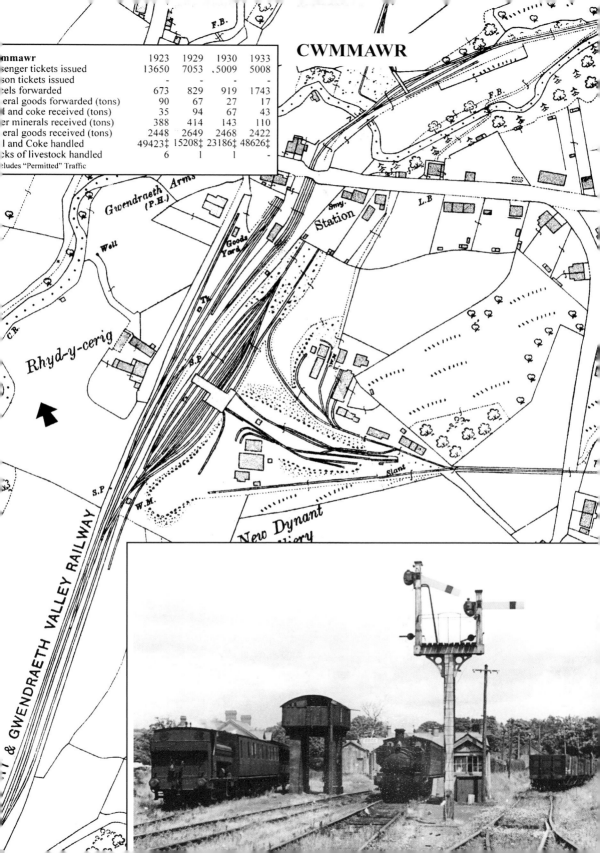

mmawr	1923	1929	1930	1933
senger tickets issued	13650	7053	5009	5008
son tickets issued	-	-	-	-
els forwarded	673	829	919	1743
eral goods forwarded (tons)	90	67	27	17
l and coke received (tons)	35	94	67	43
er minerals received (tons)	388	414	143	110
eral goods received (tons)	2448	2649	2468	2422
l and Coke handled	49423‡	15208‡	23186‡	48626‡
cks of livestock handled	6	1	1	

‡cludes "Permitted" Traffic

116.   All of the four coaches are seen a few minutes earlier, before being split. On the left is part of the coal loading screens, long disused. The branch was originally supplied with 11 ex-Metropolitan Railway coaches, plus three ex-LSWR six-wheelers. These were replaced in 1939 by special low-roof coaches, built at Swindon. (H.C.Casserley)

117.   Now for two pictures from 10th July 1958, this one with the photographer's faithful Hillman 10 in attendance. This picture shows what had been the passenger platform until 1953. There were two men employed here in the 1930s. (H.C.Casserley)

118.   The small signal box was in use from 1913 until about March 1962. It had six levers. The track in the station area was not used after 1967. (R.M.Casserley)

119.   Nos 03141 and 03145 rest on 15th June 1983. The site was by then known as Cwmmawr Opencast Disposal Sidings. In 1981, over 8000 tons of anthracite had been loaded and taken south for washing. (T.Heavyside)

120.   No. 08992 *Gwendraeth* was photographed on 26th November 1985 with a loaded train destined for the washery at Coedbach. This traffic continued until 1st April 1996, lorries then being used until opencast working ceased on 23rd March 1998. The valley fell silent, but there would always be a welcome, no doubt. (H.Ballantyne)

MP Middleton Press

EVOLVING THE ULTIMATE RAIL ENCYCLOPEDIA

Easebourne Lane, Midhurst, West Sussex.
GU29 9AZ   Tel:01730 813169

www.middletonpress.co.uk   email:info@middletonpress.co.uk
A-978 0 906520   B- 978 1 873793   C- 978 1 901706   D-978 1 904474   E- 978 1 906008

All titles listed below were in print at time of publication - please check current availability by looking at our website - *www.middletonpress.co.uk* or by requesting a Brochure showing our *LATEST* RAILWAY TITLES also our TRAMWAY, TROLLEYBUS, MILITARY and WATERWAYS series